STARLIT WATERS

Bobbi Sinha-Morey

Starlit Waters, Copyright © 2024 by Bobbi Sinha-Morey

All rights reserved. No part of this book may be reproduced or transmitted in any form or by any means, electronic or mechanical, including photocopying, recording, or by any information storage and retrieval system, without permission in writing from the publisher.

Publication History:
"The Wishing Stone" & "The Amethyst Bottle," *Quail Bell Magazine*, Sept. 2023.
"The Aroma of Basil," *Nifty Lit*, August 2023.
"Tears of Surrender," *The Wild Word*, Summer 2023.
"Spirit of the Wildflower," *Tiny Seed Journal*, October 2023.
"Like a Broken Jar," *Sage Cigarettes Magazine*, January 2023.
"A Billowing Grey Shade," *Ephemeral Elegies*, Dec. 2022.
"A Pale Fire Sky," *Pages Literary Journal*, Dec. 2022.
"A Passionate Thirst," *Written Tales*, Dec. 2022.
"Two Drops of Tears," "The Sky's Failing Light," "A Tuft of Roses,"
Rosette Maleficaram, October 2023.
"Miracles," *Spirit Fire Review*, October 2023.
"Tears of the Piano Player," *Gas: Poetry, Art and Music*, March 2023.
"Evanescent Brushstrokes" to appear in *Tower Poetry*.
"The Sharp Wind," "It's No Surprise," "Wren Hill," *Winamop*, Sept. 2023.
"The Silvery River," *Your Daily Poem*, May 22, 2024.
"A Trickle of Fate" to appear in *Two thirds North*.

Cover and interior book design: Cyrusfiction Productions

ISBN-13: 978-1-957121-72-7
Published by WHP, 2024
United States of America

Dedicated to my loving husband Joe.

Golden Teardrops

The past at last so faraway
it made my darkness slight
and the golden teardrops
from heaven have cast their
light around, a rare aura
I'd never seen before, and
now in my mirror when
morning comes I see
a face that hasn't aged
and deep brown eyes that
have never lost their glow.
There is now no dream that
has ever escaped as fast as
a summer night but a glimpse
of a tea rose sunset and a sweet
symphony of wind chimes
when the day succumbs to
stars in the evening.

A Flame of Urgency

Today I wrap freedom around me like a blanket and hell will have no place to draw its finger around my heart while I smother every thought that shies me away from whom I really am. Give me a thread of light and I'll live for the soft heavens and beckoning dawns, a rush of wind I can pierce with my hand, a flame of urgency breathlessly urging me to waken with a passionate intensity every morning with ample time to unfold myself before the world, the skies a pure cottony blue. No knots inside me to restrain my soul, only the closeness of an open doorway inviting me to fly through.

A Sweet Amenity

A morning light can't say enough
now that I've evolved into a new
reality and can cast away clothes:
torn, worn-out and old, a dash of
soft beginnings scattered before
me, a sweet amenity sent in
the wind as if a street peddler
had sold me the sky and like wood
smoke it swirled through my mind.
Branches of the world hung low,
ripe with possibilities as if a breeze
had swept through the crack of
a door and I couldn't have felt
more alive, wild as the wind,
having broken away from years
that held me back, the waters
of heaven splashing over me,
a rush of life rumbling through
me.

Like Unmined Gold

The dream came again, more vivid
now, the mystic light spilling from
the heavens like the memory of
a whisper to me I'd seen before
and cherry blossoms pushing their
heads through a mesh wire fence,
a lady's slipper lost by the gateway;
and I never knew whom it belonged
to, summer in my dream always having
gone away, but I can imagine a lover
much older by now, a dignified
looking man with fine wrinkles
becoming him who must live all
alone. Once more there was a wind
making its way down the dusty
avenue of rocks; behind them not
too faraway a cold running river.
I wish I could walk there, touch
the water that shines like unmined
gold, the ardent rhythm of the sun
above it, captured by the farthest
reaches of time when I must sleep,
a region that touches your mind
with unspoken pleasure.

The Music of Their Echoes

The waning sunlight spills on
my island when there is nothing
left to cheer me and I'm left
wishing I could step through
a portal of time where nothing
can bring me as low as this.
In my mind I travel to a gentler
plane where a big sky casts its
vibrant light and never dies;
a lap-size afghan over my knees,
in my hands a stoneware mug
of sweetened tea. No unruly
noise to breach the revered
beauty of peace: an egret living
it up in the water, letting it trickle
through its wings, and I watch
as he dips his head below,
capturing its daily fish in his
beak. Hours melt away and
I listen to the mountains speak,
the music of their echoes
when night begins, cattails
lazily swaying in the wind,
and I soon find myself
ready for a sweet sleep.

A Soft Mellow Wind

I gamble on sunsets before they die, listen to the sigh of a soft mellow wind, witness the deep violet of morning glories open and close, pale white asphodels weaving so gently with their upturned faces, the hours flexing their muscles waiting for the refulgent starlight to appear in the sky, the memory of its sweet lambency peering down from the heavens. I feel the coolness of the peaceful evening when I breathe.

WHITE ORCHID

With trembling fingers
I trace the ageless path
of the sun, the shadows
of dawn having melted
away, a white orchid I fold
in my hands reminding
me of a love so true for
simple hearts and the spirit
of grace that brought us here,
the peaceful side of silence
between you and me, the future
we share that we shape everyday,
the wings of our past we've left
so far behind, the two of us like
stars that came joining down
from the night sky. I've come
so far, my thoughts unveiled,
releasing them in the mist
on a sweet afternoon.

Love Left Its Trace

You came into my life like
a warm sweet summer rain
and your time here left its
trace, a sum of hope halfway
through the year. I cherished
how dear you were, loved
passing my hand through
your soft breath, opening my
eyes every morning seeing
how near I was to you.
Never leave me alone or
I'll write a letter, let it fly
beyond the sky asking the
heavens to bring you back.
My foolish dreams were
a thing of the past but now
I breathe a vital love into
our lives and the world
has wrapped its arms
around us like never before.

Broken Flower

How do you go on when all you
want to do is hide your face under
a pillow and feel like a broken flower
in the wind? In this world I've nothing
to hold onto and in the words of a song
I keep hearing "start living for yourself."
I unveil my weary heart, surrender my
will to what keeps gripping me tighter,
not used to the morning that has no right
to begin. I long to bury my soul in the
sweet wings of an angel before she flies
away; life is for the brave who aren't
afraid of living. I put my faith in words
I can never forget, friends who carry
blossoms inside their hearts who are
only a thread of light away. Yet I've
run out of energy to keep myself alive
and I send a half whispered prayer
to God in hopes He is listening, to
let me peacefully die in my sleep
while all the others carry on living.

A Joyful Dawn

The bridge of sunlight was
always outside my window
and I'd gaze upon it as if it
held some unseen miracle
or a dream that had only half
materialized. I never counted
the hours, only the paths in
life it took to reach heaven,
and whether it pillowed
a gentle spirit I'll never know.
Yet the thought of a kind hand
lifting me from the earth quiets
my mind. There's nothing to
replace the golden threads of
a joyful dawn or a blushing
sunset when I so patiently
watch it cease. I may pause
to be invisibly swept away
into the Almighty's heavens,
a blessing to close my eyes,
forever unfastened from
the pull of the earth.

Bright As a Sunset

In the glow of a lantern
I followed the dancing trail
of fireflies, my heart bright
as a sunset, a prayer on my
lips a bare whisper to heaven,
and in the warmth of the night
I glimpsed a mere edge of
the sun as it held its breath til
the morning. No chain around
my ankle or wrist, only an
ornament I wear clasped round
my neck. The years I envision
before me and a haven I've
always dreamed for. Pearls
I have no need of, nor nickel
either, only a minimal amount
I carry over my shoulder, and
no whisper except two broken
branches in my hands. In the
soft light I fashion a trap made
out of twigs to capture a rabbit,
sharpen a piece of wood to
spear a rattlesnake for its meat.
A sentimentalist at heart, a fire
in my eyes thinking of a blessedly
peaceful home in a faraway land.

Shelf Life of Hope

The shelf life of hope doesn't last for very long; it has to be revived by the sun, grazed by an angel's feathery wing, held in the air to feel the rush of wind, be embraced in the warmth of day, lifted like a bird testing its wings. Hope is such a changeable nature; it has to be watered and soothed by a gentle hand or by God's loving touch til it grows silently all on its own, buoyantly waving like a candle's flickering flame.

My Heart Like a Gosling

Like an unbroken glass
my elastic heart now mends
on its own ever since the man
who tried to crack his way into
our lives is gone. The crest of
our home could never break,
my eyelids like foldaway flowers
forever teased open by the warm
sun, my heart like a gosling
beneath a canopy of gracious
elms, always after a little attention
from my loved one; inside our
home a ceiling above us and
nothing can break through its
curved exterior, nor wrest away
the peace I hold like an amethyst
so dearly to me, having escaped
the malice from outside, wrapped
up in the interior of sweet blessings
inside my world.

Bird's Foot Hill

Quick as a swallow my quotidian life had been swept away and I'd stepped over the edge into a dream, the air around me reviving my senses, a new passage before me just lit, only idle fancies to occupy my days; even a wren had meandered this way, curiously bobbing its head, inspecting where I live on Bird's Foot Hill, he so gaily lifted in the breeze, unaware a feather had been missing, the whisper of time so lazily spent except to wade where the two rivers met; the scent of basil and mint from my herb garden I loved to breathe in. By the time early eve turned to a lavender sky the lantern on my porch was glowing inside with fireflies.

Iris

An iris grows inside her prim soul and in the glow of the morning when she leaves her house that iris inhales the wind – her pretty features lit up from the inside, and she blushes from what passes her by – strangers and bicyclists, vendors and florists; her heart a long ways from her thoughts, and she twists her straight blonde hair into a pretty bun. In her sustained time at home she teaches herself how to play chess, grows plant life and vegetables in her backyard garden, and she drinks in every drop of life, not caring if pollen tickles her nose or bruised petals in her garden litter the ground. Her passion is to rise by the birth of dawn, take her favorite walk round Fidalia Pond to the patisserie for breads, sweets, and pastries, an outing that just brushes the surface of memory when her father was once alive, her spirit filled with wonder and grew with her yearning for life and the ephemera of a slowly setting sun.

The Once Tranquil Air

Under a muted sky before my dream evaporates, the dust of violets obscures my eyes, nothing to override the bitterness that tasted like white pine bark on my tongue. There is a thief with a dark eye who has stolen a patch of my happiness and I've nowhere to go except stay hidden away, he so impatient to spy on what me and my partner have – the items we carry home; he so savagely jealous that his biting words cut the air like a blade. One time we reported him to the mobile home landlady and he was silent for two weeks. Others who overhear him skitter away in a hurry, and his only friend is forever on his side. In my opinion he is a donkey who brays at the wind, while me and my other half want no part of him. He gets cranky over the news on TV, and anything he says his wife laughs along with him. I cover my ears when I see him come out his door, he so eager to let loose and foul the once tranquil air. Me and my loved one whisper about him in the dark, a quiver of words between us and the cool air, wishing he'd go mute and let every passing day peacefully go by.

The Wishing Stone

Down the northern hill I took
the path to the sanctuary not
too faraway from where the two
rivers met, a bowl cradled on my
hip filled halfway to its lip with
illumined crystals, and a bag of
berries for sustenance over my
shoulder, a pale sky above me
slowly beginning to grow near
the day's end in eloquent, hushed
tones. And as I made my way
on foot to the blessed sanctuary
protected by a small gate I saw
the waters rising, gushing over
the top of its fountain. I knelt
down there in my wraparound
dress, whispered my wish and
a prayer, hoping my future will
soon one day arrive, bearing its
own gifts, overcoming the darkness.
In homage to the spirit who dwelled
above the wishing stone I laid my
bowl, rinsed my whole being,
my sun darkened skin in the waters
of the fountain, a silent joy spilling
over inside my soul.

Invisible Wings

In the cerulean light I gave way to its state of healing, the sun pouring down like honey and the spaces between my breaths stir a well of energy inside me, renewing the hope I'd once known and aiming my prayers to the heavens on a feathery wind, listening to its words and the way it gently speaks. Lost in a sanctuary of my own I touch the lake of dreams with my mind, a desire in my soul to recenter myself, capture in the curve of my hand the day's glow and let me heart fly with invisible wings.

Whispers At Dusk

A murmuration of starlings
roll like lazy oval fingerprints
across the sky and in their
birdspeak I wonder what they'd
say if they looked inside our
lives: the teenage girl who
cried wolf, the fifty-year-old
man who climbed over the fence,
our surly neighbor Loretta whom
no one wanted to know. And me,
never bound by the order of time,
always so safely hidden away in
my taste of solitude, listening to
the starlings' whispers at dusk
while I watch them arc paths
in the heavens overlapping
themselves in their carefree
flights, so unsuspecting of our
complicated lives.

A Darkened Sun

In the damp daylight hours after the rain has ceased I touch the glittering stained glass window and I cannot understand why I see only my shattered dreams floating back and forth across my retina imprisoned behind my eyelids, memories now hidden by a darkened sun. I remember only the red wallpaper inside my room, the seconds of wakening to the morning after, wishing my world were kissed by the unseen God, that He be the wind grazing on the water smiling at you, and my mind would begin to fly if He'd spill a little dash of hope on me.

Like a Golden Wing

A light shined inside of me
and lifted me; not in the way
the heavens could, nor a stroke
from God, not even the tiniest
breadth of light the daystar
could ever bring, but the light
inside lit me like a golden wing,
and for hours it felt as if my
depressive spirits had left me
that a loving touch could
never erase. I was high like
I'd never felt in days, a miracle
I'd hardly never expected that
birthed itself inside of me.

A Sweet Escape

The thought of a sweet escape spirited me away for the day and I found myself with the pleasures of nature. Before me a gentle light from the heavens spilled a round circle on the lake, a pale feather adrift on the water, and to cool off I walk in up to my neck, unafraid of anything, an emoji of peace I draw on the ground, alone with the silence wrapping itself like a manna around me, and in my quiet solitude I imagine myself a leaf drawn in its lazy descent to the soft earth, the color of peat. A flight of wrens spread their pinions, arcing paths in the air, birdsong piercing the heavens.

The Quicksilver Morning Wind

Last night's rainwater purls
through the gardens, bees work
the blooming aisles of roses,
and plum trees patiently drop
their seeds; the huge bowl
of the sky a home for a few
stray songbirds, sunlight
nestling in their wings while
their voices pierce the air
before they leave. The quick-
silver morning wind presses
so gently against my hands
like a thoughtful caress sent
down from the heavens. Not
too faraway the hum of ears
pass by my home, daylight
flickering on the surface of
their windows. Above me
and my home the sun's glow
is more radiant then ever,
like the fiery light of a struck
match falling upon the stillness
of my untouched garden pond.

Morning's Spirits

In the oval window of my room I wake to a sunrise in the rain that could not be outshined by the skillful beauty of an artist's hands. It was a rhapsody of vibrant arcs shaped so finely by the heavens' crystal touch that only the earliest riser would ever see, and in the patterns of the sky came the gentleness of a silent wind, and I longed for it to graze my face and chin, tilting my head in its direction, basking in morning's spirits smiling at me.

Rain's Light

In the rain's light heaven has unmasked it's soul and the lace curtains are stiff with dust ever since I'd chosen to be antisocial, left to carry out such a simple existence: my liquid assets I keep hidden away in my flour bin, a jigsaw puzzle left nearly finished while I search for the last missing pieces, an herbal sachet having lost it's scent ready to be thrown away, spare crusts of bread for when I go to the pond. In my meager life I have a mouth that rarely tips up at both ends, and I gaze at the artificial dahlias by the window as if they could half be alive. My heart leaks with loneliness while my life goes on, and on my darkest nights I wish for the tiny halo of strawberry blossoms.

A Tiny Sliver of Gold

Lost flowers of yesterday I once held so tightly it crushed their stems, their puffy white blossoms like my faith not more than dust wishing for a gentle spirit to touch and listen to them again, teach them the secret language of wildflowers til they shyly grow back again, lulled by the quiet waves of a stream, let their heads so lazily bend in the blissful peace, and like them I save up all my victories I'd hidden away and treasure what I now have; the sun above edging towards the end of the day, a tiny sliver of gold that graced my soul before slipping away.

Eternal Glow

Softly my heart awakens
to the gentle passage of
the wind and the very last
dream I'd had is now gently
folding its wings, my spirit
once again ready for living,
waiting for the pale sun to
shine brightly with every
ounce of its love, all of its
sharp rays so still in the day's
lapse of time. I never see it
move, only ascend ever
higher; and oh, it pierces
me with an eternal glow,
an ocean of the heart
unfolding joy inside my
soul.

Summer Rain

In the questing memories that seemed like a promise I listened to the dark green leaves of the tallest tree as they waved in the wind; a whole field all about me of wildflowers, a lot of them a spray of vibrant colors, me resplendent in a splash of red and yellow having been waiting here for the warm air of noon, an inquisitive wren fluttering so shyly above me, and I glimpse a girl in her teens carrying a willow basket held so delicately against her hip, gathering handfuls of wildflowers in a myriad to brighten her world, a silly girl frightened by a spontaneous shower of summer rain; it falls so rapturously upon my petals and face, and I drink it all in, every drop running down my stem; when it ends I feel so tiny and defiant, wishing it would come all over again.

The Crystal Jar

I thought of the crystal jar again
left to hold buttons pulled off
discarded clothes, an heirloom
from a deceased aunt, and I knew
I didn't want to let it go. At the
bottom of a box it had come with
some instructions that had once
been lost, but after poking around
they'd become glued to my fingertips,
and in my patch of time they'd said
"use wisely to dispel depressing
spirits." On a day when I'd been
feeling low I stole some ice water
away, dropped a rose petal in, filled
the jar halfway, stirred in a drop
of Amaretto and drank it all in.
Ten minutes passed and I felt
a sweet energy within. I no longer
wanted to lay inside my darkened
room; and as if paint had been
chipped away a tiny light begun
to shine through. It blazed inside
my heart, leaving behind a dark
miasma I once knew. A glowing
river flowed its way inside of me,
a breath of joy reviving me, and
it opened a door inside my soul.

The Tiniest Thing

The tiniest thing would brighten her day whether it be finding a paper clip so deeply hidden away or discovering silver bells inside a chest a great aunt had saved since her wedding day. Any bad news she'd shrug off like a knitted shawl, the moon casting its unblinking eye in awe when she'd sleep. She'd live her endless days without any worry that the shining sun was always in her root of sight and she'd squirrel away her list of hopes for the future, never burdened by anyone or anything; the daylight spilling its glow on her pillow and, wakening, she said, was the best part of her day. She loved the lazy descent of falling leaves, the wind that caressed her on warm days, hours of peace her silent friend.

An Invisible Drum

In the dusk of the April evening
and the descent of robins there
was reason for a daydream and
I let my mind drift in any which
way it would choose just to escape
like birds in flight – a calming of
the senses, a path of roses trembling
so happily under the sky. Just four
days ago a blue aura once appeared
in the air, my delicate heart melting
to the soft sound of the word "oh,"
and shadows that long ago darkened
my eyes were cleansed by my tears
and gently wiped away, the daily
sun carrying with it a moist wind,
caressing my spirit and skin; me
unpinned to roam as I will, my
jubilant heart beating to the pulse
of an invisible drum.

The Yellow Tea Rose

The last time I saw she wore the yellow tea rose around her neck and how much she glowed it made me yearn to have one of my own. Did she water it with her love? Did she sprinkle it with herbal tea? By the looks of it, it would brighten any worn threads she would wear, enhance her natural beauty with a buttery aura, and she'd smile at me. I wished she'd give me some seeds so I could watch a yellow tea rose grow so daintily outside my window. I'd give it milk with a dash of saffron just for that honeyed look, a hint which my friend passed on, and I saw the gleam in her eyes having given away the secret to such a prized gift. She said it gives you good spirits day by day and never runs out of hope. All alone I grew a yellow tea rose, faithfully giving it nutrients everyday under the sun. Then on a day that could last forever I found my manna when I wore the yellow tea rose round my neck for the very first time. A youthful beauty sprang in my heart and I knew only heaven could create such a rare jewel.

White Roses

On a day I rested my head
 below a red willow tree and
gazed up through its limbs
to the iris blue heavens, all
about me white roses were
kissed by the sun. I stole one
of their petals and absorbed
its essence on my tongue,
savored it like I do a breath
freshener then let it fly away
to be carried on the wind
forever in flight, a lithesome
dance like an airborne feather
carrying with it a light scent
attracting butterflies, nature's
life and lady friends.

Silent Song

Hope was like the scent of
jasmine that lived inside my
heart waiting to take flight,
and by the fist signs of dawn
came a silent song, a blessing
I had no right to expect – deer
nibbling petals of marigolds,
and roses standing there so
still as if an angel had graced
their curves with a thin covering
of gold; just a patch of light
grazing the edges of every living
gem of nature with a loving
finger.

Useful Things

No candy to thicken my waistline,
only pistachios and sunflower seeds
kept in a tin that once held needles
and pins; and in a small stack of
simple routes I wrote down by hand
to get me where I need to go and
back again. An heirloom from my
mother a gold limned jewelry case
that glistened like diamonds I had
to sell; a faux-leather jacket my
cousin once wore which I gave
a cursory look, kept it for myself
to wear every winter. The money
I'd so diligently saved after a day
inside the antique shop I'd hidden
away behind a painting that hung
on a wall spent only on useful
things and items at the market.
My own panacea for such a dismal
day-to-day life now that my lover's
gone overseas is a sweet herbal tea
to soothe me before I sleep and
I hold onto a dream that keeps me
alive: to swim in a cool river, its
water rushing over me.

Iris Rainbow

In the sole light of a candle's
flame a dark wind stole my
prayer away, my words never
to be heard by the overseer
in heaven and in the chilly night
I could see the now unlit window,
the dearest one closest to me all
alone inside a cell, a dry cold
floor below his feet and I'd been
told it's been two days they've
given him nothing to eat. I'd give
anything to see him be freed, let
such a kind man whose only
secret is to steal away without
a whisper with me. I'd be the one
to slip inside, me nimble as a black
squirrel, led by the peripheral haze
of memory all about me, and we'd
be hidden by the sky and woods.
In the moonlight only the black
eyes of a deer would see, and
the iris rainbow would meet us
by dawn.

Hardly a Green Thumb

I wish I could be as resilient
as the strong lilac tree, giver
of pollen to butterflies that
pass by. I'm not a gardener
who could cultivate all sorts
of seedlings, but I knew
a few names of plants my
neighbor behind me potted
just yesterday, and I didn't
need honey to attract feathered
friends, yet I yearned for new
flowers to freshen my window
to go with the scent of morning
air when I'd awaken, imagining
how pretty they'd look with
the lace curtains hanging above
them, and some sunny yellow
flowers in the mix; the wind,
barely a whisper, moving them
ever so lightly, and me such
a novice with hardly a green
thumb. The only thing I've ever
unearthed was the word "aphids"
that's always remained on my
tongue; my only indulgence
culled from my garden were
cherries from my tree served
with dollops of orange cream.

The Most Joyous Sound

The songbird's voice has quietly been stolen away, the unbroken aria come neither morning nor dusk. It's silent home in the maple trees, it lifts its shy head as if to question the gods. Fireflies dance curiously about the water fountain where he once alit, the star hawk slicing the sky bereft of not hearing the little bird's lovely sweet sound. Flustered, he beats his wings, circles the other way, wishing he'd spy him in flight, but no clue, no trace of him anywhere. One day between the first drops of rain came the most joyous sound, a melodic song as if it were a gift from the heavens coming from a faraway nest.

TO PATIENTLY LISTEN

How do you save a dying tree
when it's not too faraway from
the light? I've given it fresh
water every morning from my
gardening hose, grown a spray
of baby roses to brighten its
spirit, gave it a gentler nudge
so it will wish for the heavens,
listen for kind words in the wind.
I hate the thought of its lacy old
pale roots, not wanting to imagine
its slow lack of breath. I'd give it
a swift greening of leafy wings if
I could, lift its branches even
higher if I'd had the strength.
One cool afternoon I whispered
my love to it, pressed my cheek
to its waist. It once celebrated
every season, joyfully lifting
its essence so unruly in the air.
I longed for the birth of a crocus
or two having buried some seeds
in the moist ground, patiently
waited and listened to the wizened
words they whispered to me.

Isle of Light

Dying tree, listen to my voice.
I will always water you every
morning, you my faithful friend,
and I'll drink in the peaceful
silence you share with me,
the memory of the first
day I made a bed in the ground
to watch you grow. Now in this
hour pale gardenias glow between
us and over the years in our visits
we've come to know all our secrets.
I breathe in a smidgen of curiosity
just to hear you whisper the nature
of our love. Around us this is where
miracles live – in the warm air
that we share, in our isle of light,
damp buds once bathed in the soil
having sprung before us.

The Milk Glass Box

In my chosen isolation, captive
like a bug on a pin, a part of me
had died when I'd lost the only one
I'd ever loved for so long, and in
my solemn past I'd made a lifetime
decision to live out the rest of
my life all alone, living only for
the changes of the seasons,
sweeping pollen off my porch
steps that gather like thin layers
of yellow snow. All I'd ever
mastered was fastening buttons
with needle and thread, myself
not accustomed to such drudgery
and keeping the house tidy, my
world small as a snow globe save
for the days I tend my garden
watching God's spare beauty
grow – the lilacs, petunias, the iris
blades, watching each bud inevitably
unfold, and I was proud I'd done this
much, wishing I had more to live for.
There were no yard sales I used to adore,
but one day in the papers a hole-in-the-wall
boutique had opened up and, overjoyed,
I made my way to find a wonderful
honey hole filled with arts and crafts,
from brushstrokes to quilting, knitting
afghans, painting porcelain teapots;
and, inside a milk glass box, a message
that read "love is the key that unfolds
every portal."

Lost Dream

Before dawn the thought that I'd once had still burned in my eyes and I tore through the rosy cellophane of my lost dream, gazing at the piercing light in my window, and as the edge of the day grew came a pale imitation of what my yesteryears used to be, a life I'd held so closely to me, while even now it was only last night that my hope wouldn't sustain me anymore, today faced again with the intricate changeful nature of the sky, wishing for a sincere hand to hold me in the soft heavens.

The World Half Spinning

I breathe in the stillness when
the sun casts its first light and
I think of her again waiting to
sprout like a maple seed and
interact with God's world again,
she wracked so unsteadily by
dizzy spells and vertigo and two
months past with no relief in
sight, she barely able to stand,
a trembling rose. I wish I could
hold her in place with an invisible
hand, cure my friend of her malady
with fairy dust. May the flame of
heaven's light renew her stasis with
a single stroke. I imagine her captive
inside a swirling glass save for only
a bedpost to hold onto, her sedulous
diminutive footsteps when she moves
across the room. How agonizing it
must be not to stand up straight
but lay in bed with the world half
spinning, swimming, above your
head. After so long she must ache
wishing to be done with it, and
I pray the world about her at last
gets into place, her equilibrium
crystallizes inside her soul.

So Tersely Cut Away

Why do you have to stay away so long before we talk again when my only mistake was to say something so mildly wrong that blew out the candlelight at your end? Your thoughts must be more delicate than mine and in the hush of my room no stray answers come; this new memory of your absent response now lodged in my bewildered soul. It feels like a friend I've now lost not knowing if I'll ever hear from you again, your letter so softly hidden away in the drawer of my nightstand. We've become shapes in this invisible passage of time, my patience so tersely cut away, and my last thoughts of you have taken off like birds. I'll seal my words inside a wooden box, let the light of you die like the weight of the setting sun.

A Gentile Lady

It was a petite home of quiet
   discipline and the sign of an
uncluttered mind; a silent
wind against the window,
the morning sun burning away
the fog, revealing the first
blossoms on the trees. A woman
still lived here all by herself,
a rare vision of youth at the age of
sixty, leading a simple existence,
an organized life. She, who sleepily
awakens to the sound of her clock
radio before beginning her day,
a gentile lady who teaches the blind,
studies her curriculum after calming
pilates and her daily mug of herbal
tea, unfettered that she lives alone,
her idle time listening to singers of
the day on her radio. No one ever
knew that she was so meticulous her
house never gathered dust, her nylons
never run, and she always covered
herself before going out in the sun.
Her favorite indulgence came in
the mellow hours before evening
that always melted her little heart,
a bowl of French Silk ice cream.

Tracing Strands

Woken by a gentle morning,
the curtains swaying like
a dancer in the breeze,
I thought of the ardent waters
again, and how I'd love to swim
in them, such a brimful retreat
where no one nor any living
being could ever disturb
the ring of peace around me;
the wind a calming etude in
the air, a red-bellied robin
in flight; and a glowing memory
flickers inside me to renew my
senses with a light of good intent
that might bend like an aurora
so easily piercing my soul, and
I trace strands in the heavens
blissfully with its lithe manna
of golden threads sewing my
spirit with shapely hands.

Love's River

Love's river swept away
the shadows that once were
in my eyes, left me willowy
and fey while I swam in its
warm waters as coltish as
can be, only me in a pleasant
hour below the pale sky, and
when I breathed I inhaled
the scent of moss roses by
the river, blessed by the gifts
I always wore – pearl earrings
and a bracelet carved out of
ivory that I'd never let go.
I cleansed myself in the river,
filled with a passion inside
my heart that made me quiver.

Bobbi Sinha-Morey

Stolen Away

In the stillness of an hour
I'd found the perfect circle
inside my heart of inner
peace and I stared at the dusk,
a rare moment in my day, so
blissful like the intricate
indolence of a butterfly's
wings or an unveiled sun
that's never known the language
of rain, only its own inviting
light, its silent rays on the skin
of my cheek. A genuine smile
slowly grew on my lips, a quiet
joy I so seldom ever knew like
a stolen jewel. No one ever
knows how faraway I had
to go just to be alone like this;
me in such an unadorned,
simple dress, a sachet of
gardenia petals I'd kept hidden
away in my pocket so I could
release its essence, breathe
in the scented air.

Like Mist Over a Lake

Only in dreams do I see blossoms
unfold and dandelions swaying
in a warm wind, children bobbing
up and down in curling river water,
idly tossing tricolored halos like
playthings, the smalt in their eyes
so brimful, alive, populating my
dreams while I so peacefully sleep,
memories wakening from so deep
inside striking my fancy, and with
eyes closed I watched as each one
of them rose like mist over a lake
vanishing hours before I could
ever awake.

When a Wildflower is Born

Below the skies of heaven
I found myself coming alive,
the tips of my petals opening
oh, so slowly and sweetly,
red golden trees at the edge
of a forest gently bent to
lovingly look over me, and
it couldn't have been a dream.
My soul was overflowing,
the Almighty's manna spilling
over me; I was breathing, my
life beginning. To think in
the afterglow at day's end
human hands so soft and
pliant had buried something
so simple as a packet of seeds,
watered the ground, whispered
a prayer for next morning's
sunrise. My spirit had woken
to a season of peace; my
growth had emanated from
a nurturing touch. Having
been born I celebrate the earth
and sky, send a missive to
God carried on the wings of
a swallowtail butterfly.

Angel in Your Pocket

Angel in your pocket; it stuck
to me like a Christmas morning
gift, a freebie you'd put in your
back pocket or a saying spoken
by the divine. Churchgoers
would never get enough of
it – they'd pass it around like
the latest fad. It would sell
like a Cabbage Patch Doll,
handmade by the most loving
nuns who sew them matching
outfits. Lay them on children's
pillows, dispose of those tiny
envelopes filled with missing
teeth. I could think of so many
ways to make a living, a gimmick
that would stay inside so many
people's heads like hula hoops
or pet rocks, a thoughtful way
of saying I love you with such
a casual, kindhearted gift. Let
it be a line in a wedding song,
let it live on like a hymn or
carefully worded vow. It
would put a smile on anyone's
lips.

The Tiniest Arc

~~~

*M*y hopes thin as morning
mist slowly begun to stir
from inside my soul, and
I found myself awakening
just before the sun could
rise and offer the tiniest arc
of a demure smile. I let myself
acquiesce to tomorrow's dreams,
tacitly brightening to the soft
rhythm sparked by the heavens,
the imbalance of a flurry of
wind – it curled round a lamppost,
and it was the first time I'd felt it
on my skin; my window halfway
open, warm air wafting in, and
I wanted to impatiently rush
outside, tilt my head to the sky,
breathe in what it was giving me.
I captured its glow in the curves
of my heart, rejoiced that I was
here, alive, the sun-gold smell
of freshness all around me,
the sweetest calm pillowing
itself inside of me that I wanted
to share with the highest god
like a rare jewel.

A Handful of Dusk

The yesteryears of so long ago
had never been as bright as this
when all I had to do was rest my
hope on a star and patiently sleep
til the rising sun made its pinhole
on the horizon – the light feeling
of awakening as if the wings of
time had so silently carried me
and memories of a new life are
just beginning. Dreams now
capture me in their web, erase
the rusty hours, unlock the cage
door to release my thoughts
fluttering like trapped birds,
ready to flower like gentian
herbs. A handful of dusk pillows
the sky eagerly; no trace of raindrops,
only the soft edges of the heavens
curved into lace.

Season of the Heart

Before the golden scarlet light of dawn the flurry of discordant thoughts that spun in my mind dispersed like a flock of sparrows and in my window a solitary bird was joyously cleaning its wings in the fountain of water, and it lit a path into my soul, a clear blue light that begun to grow; I let it pierce my heart, brighten me with heaven's mysterious blessing, let its warm glow be a balm for me to cling to, and I begin the day so shyly, opening myself to the brimful skies, to the sweet hush of peace.

Spirit Island

I captured the lake shadows
  with my easel and paint, and
in my daydream an eastern
wind rippled the water with
its own pair of invisible wings
chasing away my low spirits
like paper doves melting in
the rain, a string of breaths
escaping me inspired by
the gentle subdued beauty
of the heavens beckoning
my curious spirit to move
closer to them, my passion
spilling from every brushstroke,
in my heart my own spirit island.

A Silver Thread

It had been such a simple decision
to live all alone; heartbroken, yes,
but safe inside my manufactured
home with no one to bother me in
the confines of a mobile home park
community, no anomaly from three
rows away to ever annoy me,
no cunning man who would think
of separating me from my money,
my only means of security. And
in the powerful light of the sun
I've never been supine but active
as the days and years wear on,
enlightened by this stage in life
subsisting like the hum of a bell,
no longer afraid of anything or
anyone, close to the only friends
I can count on one hand. I've been
spilled over with love only once,
my love whose absence I'll endure
forever, but now it's my solace
that keeps me in place, one which
God is free to enter, and when
I awaken in the next morning's
silence, an even peaceful dawn,
last night's raindrops are still
on my window, and they glitter
like a silver thread.

Glass Dove

Its unbreakable spirit shaped
in a soft wind, a portion of
its delicate beauty carved
by so many lives. To know
the glass dove is to touch
it's feathered plumage and
to pass your hand through
its silent breath. When
the sky opens the glass
dove lies so still in the day
star's crest of light, the snow
having fallen gently on
the ground, the heavens
reflected in the eyes of
the dove, unaware for it
never sleeps, only lays so
peacefully in its bed of
red blossoms.

So Untouched by the Wind

The words of the most beautiful song I'd ever heard struck in my heart like a bell from so faraway; it was to find a way to hope again after knowing for so long the ring of negativity that kept pinching my heart and my will shrunken from years of obedience. To think I used to pray and a cruel hand had broken me in half. Now, my spirit trembling, I'd discovered the foundations of my soul. I'd separated the shakable from the unshakable so my only self could strongly stand still – not to waver or cringe from the light, to do so unaided by God and move towards the future that awaits me. Inside a home I used to only imagine, I now love to see pear blossoms so untouched by the wind outside my window.

A Pleasant Chap

He didn't do much but grew
the spare beginnings of herbal life
in the moist soil of terracotta pots,
caress the smooth motion of wet
swirling clay to make urns, earthenware,
a new perch for his Burmese cat to climb
beside the trees outside and he loved
collecting fine rocks, polishing them by
the calm light in his backyard, a glass of
ice tea on a table by his side, each one he'd
palmed for life, a tranquil life at the age
of sixty; he itching to do more like hold
a paintbrush, hold a pen to write verse
and casually coin new words, a language
all his own, never having worked a day
in his life but well off, the only heir to
his parents who left him a pleasing sum.
All alone, his favorite place to read under
a willow, a sole hat that made him look
like a pleasant chap; a quiet, gentile man
to talk to, who will share his rare earth
insights with care.

The Stars Are Hidden

You had to pay him homage even though he never deserved it, who said for a handsome million dollars he'd love to shoot you dead; he, married to a skinny Filipino, Tess, whom he controlled, put her to work at the crack of light, a dead end for her with no way out, and she'd weep at night, wishing for someone to hear her words, that she was trapped in a marriage she couldn't escape, that her mother-in-law was a drug lord who worked the streets. Choked in misery with the tiny ounce of courage Tess had left, she burned like matchsticks to face the darkness, afraid of what her husband might do. He'd already said he'd take her son away she'd given him, never let her see him again, he himself with dreams of being a Mafia king. Where she is the stars are hidden and like a terrified bird bouncing off the glass she wishes she could escape from the world she's been captured in.

A Healing Light

On a cold day in the wind and rain, dressed in my windbreaker, I had a vision of where I would be so many years from now – a new world, a different life. The scars I've worn inside my heart once webbed like a road map now smoothed by a gentle hand; and like I would the Almighty I gave it a nod of distant respect. My spirit began it's own peaceful journey having been given love's first breath. I wake to the sun spilling over my bed, shining in a joyous, healing light I'd never felt before emanating inside of me.

Indelible Years

In the folded creases of morning a bird's beak taps against my window, a sole reminder that life before must go on and even though my heart is tethered by the light spilling in – a pocket of silence gathered around me, a hollowness begins to invade my soul and nothing is left for my spirit to cling to except for the viridian colors I see in my dreams, a bowl of sliced peaches, wedges of wet sunlight I cannot touch and a future light in the windblown heavens so faraway from me. In the indelible years of so long ago the pages of my past have yellowed with time and there's no path, no indication in the sun's glow of where I now should go, lost like a feather in the wind that has no direction and when evening comes sleep falls over me like a shadow.

Intricacy of Time

Sell me a daydream within
our intricacy of time and in
the shortest space in my warm
island of safety I'll paint it on
my wall in the smooth passage
of today, the cool light of the
heavens rushing through my
window, knots unfastening
themselves from around my
heart and when each morning
comes no seconds are lost
and a rainbow lit halo spills
its plump light all over us.

Two Drops of Tears

In the trickling silence I'd been
like a plum rose having been
snipped from its stem and felt
only half alive, ready to die,
having lost the only thing which
has kept me alive, afraid that
in my mind there was still
a shadow yet to see. I told
myself I may not go on, that
to wish for an eternal sleep
would be a perfect end; but,
until then, dahlias turn to grey
feathers in my dreams; and
outside, a puny hydrangea
bush is wilting and sagging
by two every afternoon.
Before my waking hours
when I make no whisper
of sound, my paling heart
so faraway from the warm
light, two drops of tears are
a gentle reminder that another
day is here and I forsake its
strong, brimful glare. I thought
my will was so taut, straight
as a clothespin, but when
the first rays spilled over me
it broke in half.

The Sky's Failing Light

It was as if she'd turned her
back on the living when I saw
her silently walking away and
I thought about what she'd left
behind – someone who loved
her who couldn't erase her
darkness away, and I think
only an angel could wake her
from the hollowness she carried
inside. I couldn't imagine where
she'd been going in the sky's
failing light knowing the sign
of hope had been stolen from
her very eyes and she'd been
staring into a different world
I knew I'd never recognize.
She'd left without a single
trace and I noticed a lit candle
left on her doorstep if by any
means she may have misgivings.
Once she had a heart that knew
how to live and now it was as
if she wanted to know what it
felt like to die.

A Tuft of Roses

I saw her again, the same
woman I'd been seeing in my
dreams, silently walking to
the edge of a pier, a tuft of
roses in her hand blown
apart by the wind, and I'd
wondered what she'd sewn
in her mind to walk the same
passage day after day, an indigo
stain left on the cerulean sky
I wished I could peel away.
She stood on the edge, her back
to me, as if she were contemplating
a fateful end to her life, and it made
me want to begin running away,
a pale yellow string holding me
so still, and in seconds she'd
slipped away, no trace of her in
the motionless river. I'd wondered
if she'd lost someone close to her,
if a patch of darkness had been left
inside her heart. At last I'd stolen
myself away, wishing I could wake
up, feathers of crows cloaking
my eyes.

PASSIONATE THIRST

A lasting love allows passion to live on whether it be the inner beauty of your soul or the love inside your heart fluttering like gypsy moths or bright thoughts that spill over in your spirit and your eyes. Think of dandelions and how each holds the shining secret of maple trees. Never lose the passion that lives on inside; seize it like it's the greatest gift to be alive; think of it as water for without it you'll only die. Imagine the wondrous feeling of the wind wrapping itself around you, holding you captive in it's warm splendor, and read the map in God's hand, listen to the flowing river in the privacy of a dream. Follow hidden paths to see where they lead, never lose your passionate thirst for living.

A Pale Fire Sky

Under the surrender of a pale fire sky, listening to the wind rippling through creeks, I quietly think to myself now that I'm past my half meridian my spirits have arisen and the brittle leaves I once crushed in my hand so many years ago have at last come to an end, my life like a half-finished quilt, and here I am, my bud of burning life, blooming so bright, my thoughts full of light and I gaze upon the rushing water, the elms so gentle and quiet I believe their words would be astute if they could speak. Nothing could inject this love into me; it grew like a precious rose ready to thrive in the warm air, breathe in God's urgent joy. Through open eyelids I see the first fine tentative flight of a wren splitting the unwinged space on its way to a dawn-dappled hill.

A Billowing Grey Shade

She stood there silhouetted
against the afternoon sunlight
as if her belief in God had been
stolen away and she could barely
warm up her grim smile. What
lay burdened inside her heart
with such a billowing grey shade?
And why did the lack of hope
veil her eyes? It felt as if she
were a woman with only half
a soul; no loving glow to brighten
her face and it made me think
she must have lead an abysmal
life and I longed to steal a rose
that blushed so radiantly, give
it to her, just to absorb all
the darkness she held inside.
With a heaviness I so suddenly
felt I quietly told myself, she
chose a long, slow way to die.

Like a Broken Jar

I yearn for yesterday's dawn
and tomorrow's dusk to hold
me tight like love does, save
me so I don't dwell in my own
self-pity, a part of me like
a broken jar that lay on the floor.
I listen to the silence of my
heart while plum trees and dirty
knees in my garden are being
torn away from me, erasing
themselves from my nighttime
dreams, and minutes stolen
away from what could've been
a satisfying life for me. Yet at
my feet, in the cleft of a rock,
my eyes linger on one small,
new-budded flower, glowing
in its own light just for me
to see.

Spirit of the Wildflower

I want the wind to caress
my every petal now that
I've woken, wish I could
fly myself away as if I were
born with angel wings so
I may see where all the
spring waters flow under
the arched wooden bridge,
let the sun stroke me with
its early morning light; me,
a damsel wanting the gifts
from the heavens, yearning
to be plucked from the earth
by a gentleman's hand. Oh,
what a perfect daydream;
I'd spill over with joy, tears
on my petals and stem if
it were a reality.

Tears of Surrender

Delicately as rice paper the edge of my heart crumbles away, knowing my prayers won't mend my only friend who's so ill she can barely walk without a cane. So carefully I help her to the river so she can be at peace with the water again, let the sun glaze upon her skin, wishing she could float, gently move her limbs, me watching her since I know how to swim, thinking I'd do anything just to hear her spirited laughter, and if her tears of surrender ever stained her cheeks my soul would weep. I've known her for so long – on the ranch, in the city, and now the farmlands where she stays for keeps. Her red dog in the yard, a bounty of trees and vegetables she grew with her own hands, her future dependent on the only choice of luck while she lives on prayer and the best medicines to help keep her alive, hoping her overseer won't keep her out of heaven, for like me she is meek. It would cut me in half to see her go; it would dislodge me. I didn't have the pureness of her faith, but in my solitariness I set adrift jasmine petals on the water, and watched them lazily spin.

Tears of the Piano Player

As if emptiness were spilling through
of the life she never had – no tie to
the future to offer her a drop of any
hope, you could hear the loss of her
dreams in the keys and chords she
played; a stunted life at the age of
twenty-one because no one would
let her grow, and all the time she
grew as a child in her ears she'd
only hear the word "no." To this
day if you see her under the open
sky you could pierce the veil of
her saddened nature; never a sign
of the slightest smile on her pretty
face, only shadows in her eyes
concealing memories past – a tongue
so selectively mute that no secrets
could ever spill through. An introverted
girl with little personality; yet on rare
days an expressive face would shine
through. If she ever dared whisper
a prayer to heaven it would've been
snuffed out by a rush of wind,
making it only halfway there.

A Silent Rose

One by one when everything you've ever longed for is denied your hope lies dead inside your soul, and when I think of the darkness that weighs my heart I find little use in being alive. Carrying a slim wooden marker in my hand I make my way to the river of the unforgiven and search for a patch of ground unfettered by any other human nor a trace of wind. Where I am a silent rose is watching me, doesn't even know my name; and in it's watchful patience I begin to dig in the ground with my gloved hands, making a burial for my bones to one day be here with a place for my wooden marker to stand erect, wait for the day my spirit ascends to the sky. For now the single rose lingers in my eyes and I wonder what would it say if it could speak as I lay my hat by the water and take a drink. Memories I've washed away from my mind, so relieved to be alone with only the deer and curtain of woods; a gun in my skirt pocket I've never used. Above me a blackbird flies so bravely low. No one would ever find me here; I left no clue when I left home, and all I have are unshed tears waiting to be released. I don't even care if God isn't there. I'll die peacefully on my own and no relatives nor wary traveler who ever knew my name will never know when I've quietly slipped away.

Unhidden Lives

On the other side of the fence
is the bitter stench of poverty:
transients and the homeless
living in tents, right here in
Oregon, just apart from the
freeway, time passing by them
so unforgivingly, the cries of
the youngest children disrupting
the air. Women enlaced with
coughs fearful one of them may
be spreading the Covid; their
voices stale, discomfort in their
throats, and they must endure
the chill in the air. Their faces,
their skin, glazed in callouses
and lax with wrinkles, after
days become like worn leather.
The men break down cardboard,
make it into signs; God so
nonchalant in thieving their
health, no idea of the caducity
of their souls. Stolen chocolate
and candy from a teenager's
lost knapsack is harmony on
a seven-year-old girl's tongue.

The Aroma of Basil

My father was once allergic to
penicillin and now I am, too, afraid
to go to any doctor and praying
I don't even catch the flu; my mission
in life to forever take care of my
fatherless children. In my extra time
apart from the cooking and cleaning
I'd be the fixer-upper of the family,
calking windows, patching the walls
where there were holes, connecting
electronic wires, finding just the right
batteries for flashlights and radios.
I'd nearly forgotten the scent of tea
and roses, the feel of ripe fruit,
the time my teenage daughter showed
me how to use a Bunsen burner.

I'd relish every spare moment I had,
even the time I got sick and my
youngest learned how to make
chicken noodle soup, brought me
a bowl when I was in bed. She
laughed herself silly when I told
her I taught the cat how to yawn.
As my children grew life became
easier; and still I worked at an Arts
& Crafts shop. I practiced needlepoint
at home, careful not to prick my
fingers. One day the aroma of basil
came from outside my kitchen
windowsill, and I breathed it in,
the scent so gently lifted in the breeze.

THE AMETHYST BOTTLE

The amethyst bottle sat
cradled in a velvet-lined
box and, if you touched it,
a pristine white light would
stream from it, glowing;
a spark at its center would
reach into your heart and
wake you up, the scent
of pressed petals and its
emanating warmth will
untie any knots that may
be inside of you, loosen
your spirit like the subtle
stalk of a blossom. Graze
it with your thumb when
the morning star is at its
highest and you will see
tears of diamonds spilling
from a nun's hands.

Traces of Dawn

The birds were silent today
as if a long minute hung in
eternity and, maybe now,
my life will be uninterrupted
and I'll live out my life in a
forever waking dream; just
turn the key and the traces
of dawn are worth waking
up to. Only last night a gentle
God gave me hope to wear
inside my heart and it erased
the face of my past, my future
there for me to cling to, my
shy soul everyday breathing
in the air and the light scent
of blooming Japanese flowers
while a protective, invisible
hand showed me the way,
a quiet spirit teaching me it's
okay to love again and to
slowly unlock the door after
years of no trust, healing
energies nudging me, guiding
me dream after dream.

What Daylight Could Reveal

My heart flew when I heard the whispers of the stars and where I wakened by the misty half-light of dawn I remembered what I knew. They were the words of patience, the flow of time pausing just long enough for me to see the beginnings of another life spreading itself right before my eyes; no eclipsing of the light, no strict godly hand to wrest it away from me, and it lit a fire in my heart urging me to capture what the daylight could reveal – a gentle wind, the birthing of a butterfly, the essence of a miracle all because the sun emerged from its opening to say hello, beckoned me to listen to earth's unfettered song. I wanted to touch what was given me, cherish the spill of light from the heavens as if it were honey.

Palimpsest

A light flickered on inside of me and I yearned for the soft textures of a dream, faraway from the edge of an unforeseen fate; and I long for the whisper of water, the hush of a bird's wings. I leave half-moons behind, my worst anathemas hidden away by ice and shadows, the years separating me from any vice. All I've ever hoped for is a palimpsest, let my thoughts flow like an idyllic river and be breathless – full of passionate intensity, the hush of night and the cycles of fireflies above me.

A Wilting Rose

Alone in her silent home with murmurings of the years behind her reaching her ears the widow having never recovered from her loss timorously lingers day after day; this morning eyeing the light reflecting off her crystal rosary and with a shaky hand grips her car keys again, her only desire to drive away into the distance as if she could go anywhere inside her mobile home park, and she retraces every street, never stops to say hello to anyone and no goal in mind but to drive in her undisturbed solace admiring the homes and well kept front yards on each side; she a hermit, an elderly citizen with strands of a malady inside her head; and as she drives as such is her daily routine, she makes a stop every time by the clubhouse – not to go inside, but to park near the landlord's drop slot where everyone deposits their rent checks, but she is there to sit with a lit cigarette and listen to classical music – Brahms, her favorite, on the car radio; her life filled with nothing but to traverse the streets and curves as she please; no simple changes nor new directions to alter her life, not a single thing to break her routine, she a wilting rose growing grey around the edges til she slips away, and no one will ever know.

Evanescent Brush Strokes

In a little dirt-blown town I never lived alone all because I was someone who needed propping up in my life while I held on to scraps from my dreams, added up my dollars and change for a box of vanilla sandwich cookies just so I could steal away, wishing I could lace up my own pair of wings and fly away to a different land. I secretly write down my hopes for the future, stow them away inside a used box as if they were fossilized ferns. It was only me and my mate, the two of us like a pair of mirrors. Together we'd memorize the language of birds, erase the grey matter in our lives, the sky above us upholstered in blue. We smoothed our edges daily every morning just after we'd wake up. We'd drive in mist deep into the hills til the sun would finally break through, and we'd share a sandwich by a shady oak tree, exchange thoughts in the sweet afternoon. Years upon years we'd remained intact, our lives so much the better that we'd let no one budge us apart; both of us artists devoted to our crafts til evening comes, evanescent brush strokes spilling into our lives, and each passing day we hold on to what binds us.

Broken World

How do you mend a broken world
when there's so little left to subsist
on and my three children believe
their father will never be coming
home? I sell my china just to live
on, the paintings on the wall Aunt
Agnes handed down. I had no idea
how overwhelming it was living
like this; me at thirty-five and worry
lines are beginning to show on my
brow, sacks under my eyes from
the toil of everyday life I hate
the taste of Spam and sardines,
and I wait til the end of the week
for my check from the thrift shop,
buy squares of chocolate so my kids
can live a little, repair the living room
windows because of the rapscallions
who leave their chalk art on the streets
and the sidewalks. A rustling whisper
tells me to focus on what there is left.
I'll never ask for a handout again from
my brother who banned me a long time
ago for revealing a secret, and I look
at the threadbare clothes my children
have to wear. Fifty dollars will do
come winter for mittens, and my
sewing machine still barely works
for what fabrics I can find. Silence
is such a powerful word; I've never
complained once, only opened
the door an inch or two to breathe
in the scent of lavender that comes
in on the wind.

A Crumpled Rose

Her face was like a crumpled rose, a spinster who lost her loved one many long years ago, the sounds of passing cars like the tines of forks dragging along her nerves. She can't convince her fingers to move like they used to, gardening so alien and tough on her it's drudgery everyday; she an old lady, and beauty sadly never sweetened her features, her golden years having shown no sign of kindness but left a twisted look that made onlookers either beware or have pity for her. On a day when the sun only half lit the earth she seemed so bereft as if what spun in her mind were an algebraic mystery; her skinny figure that could wrinkle so easily, and the only thing she ever wore was a scarlet rose on a chain round her neck. I suspected she was living out her life friendless and in misery, no one to leave a sweet caress on her upturned chin, no whisper of kindness to ever reach her ears. How did she live, I often wondered, her spirit waiting to depart and erase itself into the sky? No one to pay homage to her, only me. One day when she wasn't around I left a handful of lilacs on her doorstep from my garden, hoping they would brighten her soul and lift her eyes towards heaven.

Scarlet Parabola

Alone with a tin of sardines
and leftover two day old green
beans, enemies were coming
from two states away to take
over territory like ours if they
can, me left with a cousin who
must wear a back brace, needs
help moving around, the battery
inside our radio nearly dead.
I watch the clock in the hallway,
knowing I must take the long
walk to bring home our rations
from the grocery, just the four
of us growing skinny, making
sure each one gets a morsel.
One of us got shot just two
months past – a crudely made
marker behind our house in
the dead vegetable garden,
an homage of redolent flowers
in a bowl-shaped scarlet parabola
before her marker. I'd once stolen
from her a diamond I put in my
pocket to later sew into my pillow,
and there were times I would've
loved to leave on foot all on my
own, find a fantasy home where
a lady with beautiful red hair
made fresh blueberry pie, and
thoughts of it spun in my mind.
Once just a month and a half
ago I'd had the chance, and time
had been such a slippery thing
that I lost hold of what I had
and it sailed out of my hands
forever, leaving me to dream of
something I'll never live to know.

A Trickle of Fate

Slight as a pinprick I'd been reminded again of a dear friend whom had underwent an open-heart surgery, a senior citizen nearly eighty whom me and my loved one had grown to know so well and the thought that he may not live through it shattered my prayers as if no tears, no deft hands could mend him, he like a broken chessman. A pair of threads tied my heart in place, left me alone with hollow evenings, and a pale light threatened to flicker out inside of me; my world upended like a teacup, my thoughts nearly vocalic, the many tense and careless inflections that now inhabited me. Nothing more than a trickle of fate tapped at my window and now all I ever hear day after day is a sheaf of whispering leaves and my spirit has become like scratched leather. He may not last long in this life and if he is lifted up past the clouds I'd had seen the truth in God's eyes; my world would be so thin and words would lay so heavily upon my tongue. Above me outside my window is the wintry blue sky and I picture my hope like a porcelain pot cracked irreparably down the center.

Delicate Burning of My Heart

As if an angelic light had been stolen from my life I palely realized what I hoped for the most will never come again, the most delicate burning of my heart wasting away any wishes I've ever made. Open air is for the living, not my enervated hushed soul while I impatiently sew my prayers together, left with the smell of dusty velvet and time I put away for the drudgery it takes to carry on living and whether it lasts or silences me I'll dolefully wait. I used to tie knots in the half-lives of blossoms, paint tomorrow's sky in my dreams. My days are strung together listening to the wind lay bare the willow trees.

ONETIME MIRACLE

No miraculous luck will ever
fall in my lap again; it had been
a onetime miracle as if there
were a limit set in heaven.
I had cried the day it came and
now it felt like the sting of a wasp
knowing that my only dream like
a red diamond had been crushed
to bits. No ounce of hope will
sustain me, my heart left raw
and bare. I search corners for
any scrap of light as days pass,
enveloped in infinite silences
where words used to be, and
I raise my eyes to an absent god,
knowing my prayers were thrown
against the wall, the dust of my
life sobering me to stamp out
any belief that my dream will
ever happen. Remembrance
of what I once had is now
a left-over gift of the mind
leaving me impatient, wishing
I could do without. When I lay
in bed at night a lifetime of
despondency swallows me.

DOVE-GREY DAWNS

In the tenebrious days before me
it was a dream that so barely
survived til its tiny flame silently
died and I hardly knew the feeling
of being alive anymore. Dove-grey
dawns replaced the sun; an unseen
finger opened the door to let out
the tears, the future no longer
awaiting me anymore; only an
invisible pin fastening me to
the present leaving me enough
room left to breathe, but no space
to be wild as the wind as I used
to be. I grew used to the movements
of existence, a burden that felt like
the longest stage in life before death.
There were no panoply of highlights;
they were hidden away from me like
untouchable, glimmering red jewels.
If I even escape this meager life with
nowhere to go except to grow old
I'd reach for the only hand that had
given me love and remember its
light, carry it with me til I peacefully,
forever, close my eyes.

Like Starlit Waters

Sleepless I waited til the morning star before dawn was spilling over, watching through my oriel window the flurries of fireflies as they spun in the air, and thought about her again, my best friend I'd fallen out of touch with nearly twenty-one years ago, wishing I knew what she'd be doing today. Just a day ago I'd sent a kind card her way with my thoughts inside and my e-mail address hoping to hear word from her, such a dear friend, and she lingered in my heart like starlit waters, a well of hope fluttering inside of me like a pair of wings, aching to know if she were still there and what she would say, her spirit like a budding dahlia or iris who drew in the sun, and during the time we were together our lives were graced with chatter and laughter as if God had brought us together. What swept us apart were the fingertips of untrustworthy souls that brushed into our lives. I'd awakened after the darkness had dissolved, and the plum joy in her heart was a gift she always gave away. In the stillness before the beginning of the new day I lit a jasmine scented candle and made a wish.

Songbirds Streaking Over The Hills

Deep in me dwelled a sliver of regret
that I'd confided to her and now it's
been a month that she's stayed away
I thought of writing to her again on
the first of May but I didn't know
where to start; she a cousin and friend
from so faraway, and I've never felt
so alone before. How do you ever
know for certain if you're doing the
right thing? It's like a nick in your
heart, and in my dreams I see the walls
in my room fading away. Weeks ago
I'd gaze upon songbirds streaking over
the hills, and their beautiful sound
hung in the air so I could hear every
note. Now when I wake I see a motionless
river and the brightness I once knew
has slipped away. I'd had so few friends
in my life, the kindest ones I'd clung to
the most. All by myself I hear the floors
creak, let the morning light quietly spill
in through my window, eschew prayers
that are so alien to me; and when I sleep
at night I barely remember my dreams.
The only joy I have left to look forward
to is the way the wind gently caresses
the linden trees.

Like a Sunrise Prayer

Just to smell life again my heart
lifted like a sunrise prayer, and
I yearn to bottle wind just to
save it, witness a hummingbird
flutter its wings, take refuge in
the shade of a tree, cradled near
its trunk as if learning to breathe.
I raptly gaze upon its flight,
the golden earth below, the honey
wheat field joyful under the sun
like a soul that perpetually overflows.
I listen to its motion and to its
stillness, wrapped in the warm
breath of air; grey dawn-dappled
foals before me galloping down
a perfect hill, and as the mist
unveils the brow of the world
with a freshly cooled milky
light it ignites a spark inside
of me fat as a thumb, an oil
painting imprinted on my muse,
and I've awakened for it to come
spilling through my fingertips
and my paintbrush, see flowing
imagery tumbling down, their
feathery touches alit upon
my canvas.

The Pearl White Box

I would've wept if I'd seen
those Australian opals so
carefully set in their curved
places, a gift set of them in
a petite box, a ring in the center
with a space to put one of
the opals; a precious gift my
father had given me when I was
seventeen and suddenly now it
was gone, lost in the years and
decades of time. Air, like love,
had wrapped itself around my
heart; and I knew if I ever found
it again, I'd press it so close to me
like I did the silent love for my
father. One day in a slip out of time
I'd unearthed a shiny, rich jewelry
box my mother had left behind and
I found myself crack open like an
egg at what lay inside: the same pearl
white box. Alert as a deer I breathed
in the sunlight and opened the box,
and I had no Kleenex for my tears
when I cried. Under the cushion
a crepe paper so neatly folded
stuck out at a corner and I opened
it to see what it read: let it be my love
that guides your dreams.

A Pungent Aroma

I listen to the wind grazing
the bay leaves, their green leaves
fluttering so easily as if inviting
me to draw near, making me
wonder if they may have voices
of their own, and how did they
see me so faraway on the path?
I imagined them murmuring so
lazily, the sunlight brightening
their souls, spilling on a stream,
making the water gold, and I think
to myself of the sweet daytime
when everything shines upon
the earth. Even the celebration
of life born from seeds push
themselves from underground,
layers of soil, through faces of
old pale roots just to emerge in
the inviting warmth like the birth
of delicately white baby's breath,
their airy feel so soft to the touch;
yet hyssop comes in its galaxy
of colors, its liveliness a pungent
aroma to others.

Wishing For a Sparkling Light

Memories begun turning to
dust, swirling endlessly inside
my mind that moon shadows
could never chase away; and
me, a wisp of a woman inside,
wishing for a sparkling light or
a moment of beauty I cannot
touch, and I ache for a sky painted
a delicate eggshell blue, yet what
my heart longed for the most
was a sunset on the ocean water,
a shimmering tangerine that could
only be fashioned by the hands
of God.

Shy Pearls of Noon

My thoughts unspooled in the silent rhythms of yoga and they grew like dahlias in the shy pearls of noon, a velvet umbra of a great white oak tree just over me, and I'm lost in a daydream of lavender dust, imagine it a stained map on my skin, and I trust in my dreams as if they could be the endless path to eternity. In any hour I surrender my soul like this, breathe in the timeless scents of nature carried on a soft wind.

Arc of Time

I tied a necklace of golden
   daffodils, laid it by the rainbow
stone she'd once given me and
now she had slipped away through
an arc of time and it's been months
since I've ever heard from her again.
From the smallest seed our friendship
had grown and now there's an empty
space where she used to be. No sign
that she is still there, no clue to what
was now a mystery. A quiet Wednesday
is before me again, and again it feels
as if she belongs to yesterday; no word,
no trace from her end. She a self-effacing
soul governed by a gentle spirit of the
heart, her kind nature flawless like airy
silk. Now days have been lost and it's
halfway through the year. Once she
showed me how to put my hands
together in prayer; a habit, she said,
that always brought her hope everyday
of her life. For the first time I thought
of God and asked Him to lay a little
luck on my doorstep.

A Shining Rose

Save a stitch, there's no thimble
of hope for me anymore and
the peppery scent of fading
carnations is in the air. Tucked
into the edge of my mirror is
a small note for the future,
one filled with puffs of midges
and a layer of darkness where
the bright afternoon should be.
I long to breathe in the scent
of sage tumbling in the wind
once again, but the back roads
to such an eternity are gone.
If only a whisper of lavender
dust would come my way I may
be more hopeful than I am today,
alone with a smidgen of light
from my everyday life, waiting
for a rise of elation inside my
heart. It's so easy to turn another
page, see how still the ominous
moon can be. By God's will
I'm sealed away inside a protective
shell – to be loved by Him, yes,
but no way to pass through
the window, touch the sweet
petals of a shining rose.

A Pause in the Rain

A stray thread of light
led me to peer through
the window when there
had been a pause in
the rain and in the beauty
of the heavens I'd seen
a turquoise sky and it
glimmered back at me
like the scraps of a dream;
I saw green and yellow
leaves wet with beads,
the gentlest touch of
the wind like a delicate
hand and they wavered
in their own way of
saying hello. It felt like
the tiniest gift; I could
steal away with it wrapped
inside my memory, and
I told myself I could live
like this with an eternal
light inside my soul. No
more wayward moons
at night; only a yearning
to follow my passion
into every tomorrow.

The Sharp Wind

Maybe I could find the answer why the past still clings to her eyes, why her lingering shadow casts tears on the ground, wishing she'd light up the sky like she used to. Maybe the clue will fall from her hands and she'll sweeten the time with me like she's done before. For now all I see is a slim grey veil whenever she is near and a helpless feeling inside grows not knowing how to reach her. I lay a little note on her pillow hoping the words will break through to her when all that is left is just another day staring at you. I left only half a prayer on my windowsill aching for a whisper from heaven, but soon the limit on my patience will come to an end, and when it does I'll turn my head away from the Almighty God, let the sharp wind whip at my window.

It's No Surprise

On the black canvas of my dreams
he's no longer there, and I'd give
it my implicit approval that life is
now better, the memory of him now
scattered like stale cigarette ashes,
his whispers of two-faced promises
having evaporated into the air, and
in the thesaurus of hearts he's as vain
as indecision. Sometimes the mist
gives way and I think of how damn
mean he can truly be; he with rarely
a friend in the world except me, and
he with his cruel imputations; it's
no surprise his only other friend is
in the business of swindling people
out of their money and using them.
One morning I summoned my
willpower never to call him again,
wizened by a sound mind and
patience. Lonely, yes, but a sweet
air all around me like rose water
essence.

A Brittle Rose

It wasn't like the loss of a loved pet or a lost pair of Nostroms high heel shoes, it was the absence of my brother I'd always pined for over the years. His words no longer in my morning email, his voice never there because I could no longer reach him by phone; even if I did I'd stuff my words under my tongue. I never knew if he still ever thought of me or if his Crohn's Disease made him quietly slip away; and now every passing day I have dreams of seeing him and my family in Baja California again. Would it be the same I always wondered, or would I be given a cold reception? I think of the cards I sent that intercepted him, my emails sent his way wondering if he or someone else ever read them. I breathe in the stillness of my unswept kitchen, wishing for the years or a miracle to bring us back together again. Now I look at the broken lip of my teacup, the tea inside having grown half cold, and, my head bent low, I feel like a brittle rose about to snap in two.

Swept Away Like Broken Glass

As if there were a watchful eye in the sky I'd been more aware of my every movement like setting my alarm clock for five minutes to seven a.m., adding at the top of my list to beware of our mean neighbor and always keep important documents in a tight, secure place. Impute it to God to fasten His gaze on me, make sure every detail of my life is conducted just right. Spam stored in the pantry in case of covid and famine; closely guard every cent and possession. I study my husband's daily habits of living, keep them pressed to me tightly. I chase my stress down with a cup of tea, and in my only idle minutes of time I double-check my priorities for the next day, wishing I'd have time to admire the beauty of the moon, a gift from the heavens. But I listen to the hum of silence all around me, learn the art of not being seen so I can go on, unaided with living, most of my life of no use to me as if it had been swept away like broken glass. Before I close my eyes to sleep the darkness outside reminds me of the biggest burden of all: to be practicing aloneness in a future life, a grim window I hadn't passed through yet.

I Struck a Match

At last my diary had made its way back to me, wrested from the dead person's wicked hands. I didn't miss the veiled threats, the cruelty dished out after so long, and just to be sure it couldn't happen again I stole away to the rusted can three yards away from the back of my house, matchsticks in my pocket, and no one around, not even the mendicant with prying eyes from the nearby Presbyterian church. For a minute I was seized with a sudden insight – be true to your heart, and I had been, then it damaged my life.

I struck a match, held it to the corner of my thick, thick diary, and tossed it inside the can – pale, teal smoke rising as I watched it burn, fireflies skittering about, attracted to the flames; a dark grey sky above me, and I told myself I will never put words on paper again. I'd begin a new life with no regrets this time, and I took out a palm sized envelope with a missive to God and let it burn, my words reaching heaven.

Like Faithless Starlight

In my own private Ukraine
any hope I had was trampled
to death by little shoes, my
fear like an arrow aflame
slung into the color of the night
sky, believing it would spell
an end to our country if Trump
should win again, an elegy for
nationwide peace. My only wish
is to put an end to anything that
tries to divide us, not to let
hope die like faithless starlight.
I breathe in stale air leftover by
the homeless spreading Covid
and disease, turn my head away
from politicians who make
promises frail as dry twigs.
Life could be given a turn for
the best by the grace of God's
hand and I could climb out of
the sealed shell I am in.

I'll Listen to the Pallor

In the shorelines of my sleep
hidden behind blue glass I saw
an image of myself, a white
moth twirling in the wind
having fled a broken stained
glass house, led only by
a beckoning candle, its flame
twice so shy and I'll never
forget a rainbow having
grown so dark as the night
sky, the heavens only a beacon
for the dead, a shadow fluttering
inside my eyes, fearful the sun
may never come again. I swim
in the pale blue aura that had
once been given me, no chance
for reaching out to a giving
hand, and if I die a little I'll listen
to the pallor of the following day,
my greying heart having given
way.

Golden Thread

*I*n the silence of the day I ask myself where am I going as I walk far from my home, as I cry for my future I buried today, gathering flowers that never awakened but died before morning, their heads hung over their stems, and I place them on my unseen grave, searching for echoes to lead me on a new path in life while I let time pass me by, memories that travel through the years, pinching me as they unravel inside, and in the twinkling of an eye, the sky is veiled in grey as if God weren't here, no love today. Yet I make a wish, tie it to my heart with golden thread. Night sneaks up behind me and I am barely ready for it. On the ledge of my bedroom window someone has lit a votive candle. No prayers are sent, and I long to keep my eyes open to see the world before they close forever.

Ill-Fated Misgivings

His motives were born in the makings of a raven's nest; the very individual who'd prey on you til all your money was gone. Just to think he'd dangle his own brand of bait just to tear two lovers apart. I know I'd have ill-fated misgivings if I ever went near him, and it takes no gentleman to see his interior; he's not half as sly as he thinks he is. Just to be rid of him would be a blessing for anyone, and those who think they knew him best are in danger of his true intentions. To know him well would be perilous, and for a woman to see him as a potential man she'd find out the hard way when all her savings were gone; no way of getting it back, and he'd always be proud of it when he could use someone. But he can't bypass time; his body and age are showing telltale signs. With a little luck I'll outlive him, lay my head on my pillow and sigh a sleepy sigh.

The Silvery River

In my solace I stole away
from the Tea House after
working for most of the day,
ready for an idyllic repast,
a petite basket in my hand,
my wages tucked away in
an old cocoa tin; and as
I turned left by the lane
I caught the scent of young
roses in the air, the sky once
so bright and gleaming, now
the pale hours before evening.
A bicyclist swept past me;
an elderly citizen walked
her Pomeranian. I followed
the peaceful, fluttering path
of a butterfly, and I found
my way to the silvery river.
There on the grassy shore
I pulled out my unlined
notebook, begun with
a prayer from the heart,
and drew the natural life
all around me: the flight
of swallowtails, how they
arced in the sky; the curiosity
of dragonflies in the early
illumined night.

Lavender Dreams

The sweet perfume of sliced apples gently hung about the pretty-voiced woman who lived by herself below the sun streaked sky, a day in April, her windows jeweled with raindrops while she has a heart that so quietly unfolds. Before her the present and future alternate like soothing winds, and in the tiny flame of each day's beauty she pins cotton and silk to dress patterns, bakes marble rye with her own hands, living on thimbles of hope rinsing her spirit daily, a stray light from the heavens renewing her each morning she rises, the air around her not stretching itself so tightly, and her pillow scented with a delicate beauty she loves to breathe in, a wick in her heart lit with an undying energy, a bud growing inside her when night comes, the moon slipping lower, its half-lidded eye watching over her; hope inside her soul that begins to grow, her head so blissfully filled with lavender dreams.

Before The Sun Dies

Alone in a two-star town where her dreams hide and no way to leave the scarred years behind she races shadows before the sun dies; she who aches inside a house that may crumble away from beneath her feet, moonlight illuming the dust, she tracing the cracks on her bedroom walls mirroring the ones inside her heart, she wishing for a way out, prayers swallowed in the foggy atmosphere, left with the fear she'll forever be here, feeling only her threadbare hope when she breathes; the rapture in her young heart when the boyfriend she loves flees with her in the end so faraway that no one will know where they are. With rolled-up sleeves they plant and water rows of seeds when they begin their new home, the fragrance of the night wrapping the spirits of their new lives together like beveled diamonds carved by angelic hands in the skies of heaven.

The Silver Rose

Before the wedding my nephew beneath an arbor burst into tears saying his mother, my deceased sister-in-law, should've been here to see my niece marry; and now, in spirit, my former sister-in-law Janie was nothing but the warm morning air before my niece and her groom could go down the aisle and take their vows. I stared at my nephew and at first it hurt almost like a bee sting – the air around me thickening, and breathing becomes a choice. I trembled inside, and my hands holding a Styrofoam cup of juice begun to go numb. My brother's new girlfriend beside me, and I trace the strands of daylight in her locks of dark hair; she who poised herself so well, like a blossom or an iris, and she stood there slowly sipping her green tea, shades of deep yellow shuffling in the wind, the flower girl wandering around, nothing more than a five-year-old, carrying a small willow basket cradled in her hands, a bevy of showy flowers stuffed together, some leaning over the sides. She stops for a minute, sees the tears spilling down my nephew's face, and hands him a silver rose, a wee wish that he'd brighten, wipe the tears from his eyes.

The Tiniest Gift

A loss that carved a hollow space inside my heart will never be replaced again, no handprint of the sun on a curve of the lavender hill will ever reawaken my dying spirit again, and the dream waves in the fingers of my sleep no longer caress me anymore. The world doesn't know of my empty hope and the dust in my mind begins to grow. I barely move, unable to slow the passing of days, and I think of the rosebuds in my untouched garden dead in the dry soil. I can only wish for the tiniest gift, that I'll learn to fly, escape the earth that fastens my feet, wish for a sweet eternity where no dark light nor chill wind can ever pierce me.

Patterns of the Sun

My spirit in the stillness of the morning light was like an orchid to be kept under glass, no ripple of the wind to brush my cheek, me afraid to lose a dear friend after so long, and the thought of it makes me quiver, presses me in my silence to be meek; my aura once a delicate pale blue now mute as the color of a moth. I lay so still taking in the patterns of the sun, wishing I could send a prayer before it's been forgotten, and I breathe in the thin layer of dust that lingers in my home. What little faith I have left reaches out its hand for a warm drop of hope the sky gives while I lay here fastened in bed, wishing I didn't have to be forgotten and alone.

Prayers at Dusk

By noon a dark patch clouds
the sky, the unfettered wind
marking its path above our
house on an off day in our lives
when our words didn't go right
and the sun in my angry eyes
couldn't wipe the tears away;
an oseir basket that lay tipped
over on the rug, the two of us
separated in different rooms,
me left with the feeling of
aloneness deep inside, and
a passing thought that someday
the walls may close in on us.
I didn't go into denial knowing
the space between us was my
fault, my guilt feeling like
penitence, interrupted by
a minute of blessed relief
when the sound of laughter
cracked the air, but the tide
of it didn't last for very long,
the well in my heart of silent
regrets by day's end that not
even prayers at dusk could
mend.

The Winds of Forever

In the morning I heard
the sound of her wings;
she was there to waken me,
to take me away to a sun filled
land where she'd be my only
friend, a reprieve to last forever
from the endless unbroken task
of living, and for me it was
a blessed relief, an idyllic peace,
a glow still in my heart to keep
my spirit alive, so faraway from
the magnetic pull of the earth.
Memories still fastened inside
my heart, and now only a sense
of letting go and gliding into
a more featherlight existence;
no trace of how I once lived.
No dream, nor reason nor wish
to bind me, only a portal of air
so God can see into my soul,
the winds of forever wrapping
themselves around me and
acquiescing to their touch.

Like Soft Twin Gazelles

The memory of her belongs to
yesterday, a dear friend I once
knew more precious than silver,
a timid rupture of my heart at
the thought of her again, a lily-
handed young blonde woman
who now lives elsewhere under
the teasing sun, time having
swept past us like soft twin
gazelles, and in my silent repast
I imagine she is like an untouched
white rose, a flower of the year,
gaiety once on her tongue who'd
been closest to me til the very end,
a part of me now like a candle
absent in flame. Now what
remains is God's hand nudging
me while it's so hard for me
to unbearably move on.

The Last Song

Scientists could've never predicted the end of our lives and it's all because Putin wears a cryptic grin, an impudent being aiming his sights on America, and life as me and my loved one know it will be gone. There will be no martins or deer in the woods, no more visions of nature's beauty like the lakes that remain in our memory, wild plums that grow ripe on the vine. I think of racing in the sun, have the sweet taste of blackberry pie on my tongue before my spirit must move on. We play jazz in the day, laze in the patio with a favorite book or two, while away the last of our treasured time searching for rock, take side trips in the car for half a day, breathe in the warm air, be like gleeful kids going after a bevy of sweets. We think of the best movies to see before we die. I wished for the sparkle of rain on the window, yoga practice in morning's light, but what I have left to me are only minutes of my time so I steal away with a CD, listen to the last song I'll ever hear before I'm in heaven: "Suddenly" by Olivia Newton-John.

A Mellow Hymn

When the last teardrop falls
from heaven a new day has begun
and in the sweet air around me
I hear a mellow hymn and it
felt so idyllic and new. It evoked
a memory of a friend I once knew
who lived on Opal Road and she'd
invite me inside her home where
she'd offer me tea and over the years
I'd found a place for her inside
my heart. Indoors she lead such
a tranquil life; and the quieter
I became the more I could hear her
heart speak. She a delicate girl who
lived for autumn skies and giving
her love to every living thing. She
developed a faith of her own to be
kind to others, selflessly gave away
the bevy of herbs and vegetables
she grew with her own hands, and
she'd give her love away to those
who were closest, saved all her
hopes for Sundays, lived with
a sweet passion everyday.

ALCHEMY OF THE SUN

In the ambient alchemy of
the sun I was left at the edge
of a dream and a light flickered,
urging me forward to a future
I'd had no clue of before, and
between me and the sky there
was only the warm air to touch;
it traced my heart, awakened
my soul, and I breathed in
the hope of a joyous tomorrow.
I was quick to follow the path,
nothing to separate me from
what I believed in and my
solitary life, and I blessed
the Almighty who brought
me here. I sent a whisper to
the heavens for such a gift
so spontaneous and ripe:
one last road in my life
sweetly carved out by
the hands of time.

A Brightness That Lies So Still

I listened to the endless music
inside my dream and never
wanted to wake up; just let my
heart stir to the sweet melody
while I peer through the clear
glass before me of an honorable
and graceful future world where
it's easy to live, breathe in
the earth's healing nature, let
the unbroken words of the music
reach deep down inside my soul;
it is a brightness that lies so still
like a source of purified water
and like a lazily nurturing spirit,
yet it could be so easily lost like
a loose feather. Trap its essence
instead and may it last forever.

The Eternal Dawn

The afterglow of the soul
is what my mind has painted
for me today – the eternal
dawn of the minutes and hours,
whispered prayers slated for
heaven, our spirited hearts
happy all day while we watch
the ascent of the sun, feel
the tug of a warm breeze.
No silent laughter, no droopy
blossoms; we soak up new
memories before the old ones
can ever drift away. Only
the youth and the wise cherish
what we have today; love fills
the air, our faces and eyes.
We breathe in hope that has
banished our tears, given us
dreams we believe in and
touch, a beautiful lifetime
we shape everyday.

My Heart So Ripe

Glistening water reminded me of a blessed, timeless passage of peace when a rainbow painted the sky and my hope floated in a soft breeze, a gift from the heavens to glow so idyllically under the sun and no one can ever steal away your Zen. I live in a stream of daylight, my heart so ripe I'll never let go of the joyous river that flows deep in my soul.

Miracles

Staring beyond the blue veil of the heavens I ask myself where do miracles come from if they're so unexplained? Are they sprinkled from God's invisible hand? So unseen in the skies above, yet we see them right here on earth; no magic dust, they're unexpectedly, mysteriously given birth, and in the center of your soul it's a wonder, a climax you never forget; you carry it everywhere with you and never let go. Where they come from no one knows, but it leads you to your own personal paradise in heaven, and sharing it with someone helps make it real. Hold onto one when it materializes before your very eyes; it will last you for the rest of your life.

About the Author

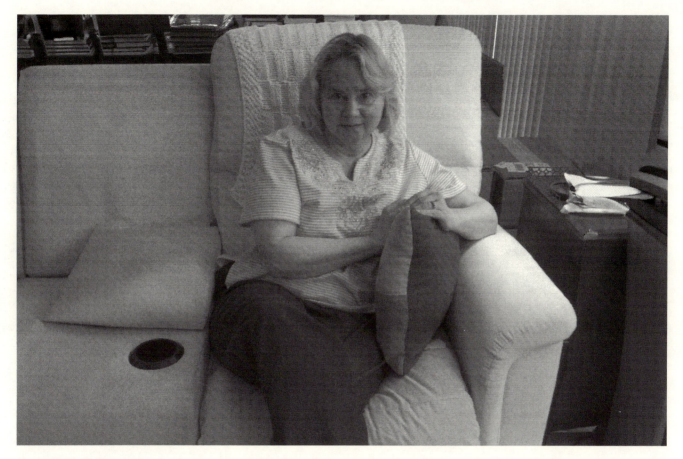

BOBBI SINHA-MOREY lives in Central Point, Oregon with her husband, Joe Morey, where she writes poetry in the morning and at night, always at her leisure. Her poetry has appeared in a wide variety of places such as *Plainsongs, Pirene's Fountain, The Wayfarer, Helix Magazine, Miller's Pond, The Tau, Vita Brevis, Cascadia Rising Review, Old Red Kimono*, and *Woods Reader*. Her books of poetry are available at Amazon.com and her work has been nominated for The Best of the Net Anthology in 2015, 2018, 2020 and 2021 as well as having been nominated for The Pushcart Prize in 2020. In addition, her website is located at http://bobbisinhamorey.wordpress.com.

Made in the USA
Middletown, DE
14 April 2024

52991845R00078